Audition Songs Number One Hits

Published by
Wise Publications
8/9 Frith Street, London W1D 3JB, England.

Exclusive Distributors:
Music Sales Limited
Distribution Centre, Newmarket Road, Bury St Edmunds, Suffolk IP33 3YB, England.
Music Sales Limited
120 Rothschild Avenue, Rosebery, NSW 2018, Australia.

Order No. AM91540
ISBN 0-7119-3762-1

Compiled by Lucy Holliday
Cover design by Fresh Lemon

CDs recorded, mixed and mastered by Jonas Persson
Backing vocals by Elly Barnes

CD BACKING TRACKS

Disc 1

1. **Don't Cry For Me Argentina** (Lloyd Webber/Rice) Evita Music Ltd.
2. **I Will Survive** (Perren/Fekaris) Universal Music Publishing Ltd.
3. **A Woman In Love** (Gibb) Warner Chappell Music Ltd./BMG Music Publishing Ltd.
4. **The Winner Takes It All** (Andersson/Ulvaeus) Bocu Music Ltd.
5. **There Must Be An Angel (Playing With My Heart)** (Stewart/Lennox) BMG Music Publishing Ltd.
6. **China In Your Hand** (Decker/Rogers) BMG Music Publishing Ltd.
7. **Eternal Flame** (Hoffs/Steinberg/Kelly) Universal/MCA Music Ltd./ Sony/ATV Music Publishing (UK).
8. **Show Me Heaven** (Rifkin/Rackin/Mc Kee) Famous Music Publishing Ltd.
9. **Nothing Compares 2 U** (Nelson) Universal/MCA Music Ltd.
10. **I Will Always Love You** (Parton) Carlin Music Corp.

Disc 2

1. **Think Twice** (Sinfield/Hill) Mrs/Chrysalis Music Ltd.
2. **...Baby One More Time** (Sandberg) Zomba Music Publishers Ltd.
3. **Don't Speak** (Stefani) Universal/MCA Music Ltd.
4. **Perfect Moment** (Marr/Page) Chrysalis Music Ltd.
5. **American Pie** (Mclean) Universal/MCA Music Ltd.
6. **Can't Get You Out Of My Head** (Dennis/Davis) EMI Music Publishing Ltd./Universal/MCA Music Ltd.
7. **Freak Like Me** (Numan/Hanes/Valentine/Hill/Collins/Clinton/Cooper) Universal/MCA Music Publishing Ltd/Notting Hill Music (UK) Ltd.
8. **Heaven** (Adams/Vallance) Rondor Music (London) Ltd.
9. **The Tide Is High (Get The Feeling)** (Godfrey/Padley/Holt/Barrett/Evans) Sparta Florida Music Group Ltd/Universal Music Publishing Ltd.
10. **Beautiful** (Perry) Famous Music Publishing Ltd.

London / New Yo… …n / Madrid / Tokyo

Disc 1

In C major

In A minor

In E♭ minor

In G♭ major

In A minor

In B major

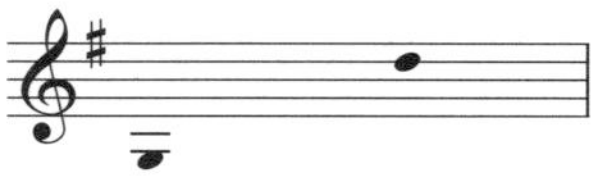

In G major

In A♭ major

In F major

In G major

Disc 2

In F major

CD Track 1

Think Twice

Music: Page 58

In D minor

CD Track 2

...Baby One More Time

Music: Page 63

In C minor

CD Track 3

Don't Speak

Music: Page 68

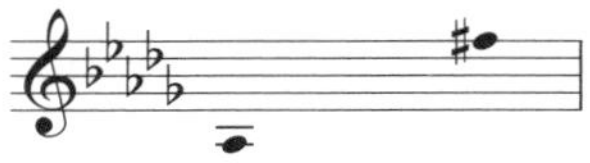

In D♭ major

CD Track 4

Perfect Moment

Music: Page 74

In A♭ major

CD Track 5

American Pie

Music: Page 80

In D minor

CD Track 6

Can't Get You Out Of My Head

Music: Page 86

In B♭ major

CD Track 7

Freak Like Me

Music: Page 91

In E♭ major

CD Track 8

Heaven

Music: Page 96

In C major

CD Track 9

The Tide Is High (Get The Feeling)

Music: Page 103

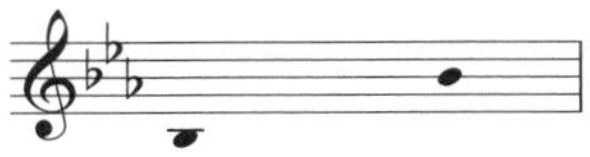

In E♭ major

CD Track 10

Beautiful

Music: Page 108

Don't Cry For Me Argentina

Music by Andrew Lloyd Webber
Words by Tim Rice

F/C
G7/C
ea-sy, you'll think it strange When I try to ex-plain how I feel, That I
C
Am/C
still need your love af-ter all that I've done: You won't be - lieve me,
D
D/C
All you will see is a girl you once knew, Al - though she's dressed up to the
G/B
D7
G
C
nines at six-es and se-vens with you. 2. I had to let it
F/C
G7/C
hap-pen, I had to change; Could-n't stay all my life down at heel: Look-ing

C
Am/C
out of the win-dow, stay - ing out of the sun. So I chose free - dom,
D7
D/C
G/B
Run-ning a round try-ing ev-ry-thing new; but no-thing im-pressed me at all, I
Slow Tango feel
D7
G
C
F/C C
nev - er ex - pect-ed it to. Don't cry for me Ar-gen - ti - na, the
F/C
C
G
truth is I nev - er left you: All through my wild days, my mad ex -

Am Cmaj7 Fmaj7 F6 F
-ist-ence, I kept my prom-ise, Don't keep your dis-tance.
C F/C
3. And as for for-tune and as for fame - I nev-er in-vi-ted them
G/C G7 C
in: Though it seemed to the world they were all I de-sired. They are il-
Am/C D7
-lu - - sions, they're not the so-lu - tions they prom-ised to be, the
poco rall.
D/C G/B D7 G
an-swer was here all the time I love you and hope you love me.
ten.

Slower
C
F
C
(bouche fermé)
Don't cry for me Ar-gen - ti - na.
Mm
p
G
Am
Cmaj7
F6
dim.
pp
ppp
Tempo I°
C
F/C C
F/C
C
Don't cry for me Ar - gen - ti - na
the truth is
I nev - er
left you:
All through my
f
G
Am
Cmaj7
Fmaj7
wild days
my mad ex - ist - ence,
I kept my prom - ise,
Don't keep your dis - tance.

Fmaj7
Em7
Have I said too much? There's no-thing more I can think of to say to you
pp colla voce
ppp
Fmaj7
But all you have to do is
rit.
a tempo
C
F C
look at me to know that ev-'ry word is true.
ff
p molto Ped.
F/C
C
N.C.
ten.
G
Am
Cmaj7
Fmaj7

I Will Survive

Words & Music by Dino Fekaris & Freddie Perren

Am
Dm
G
back from out-er space I just walked in to find you here with that sad
me, some bod-y new, I'm not that chained up lit-tle per - son still in love
Cmaj7
Fmaj7
look up-on your face. I should have changed that stu - pid lock, I should have made
with you; and so you feel like drop -pin' in and just ex -
Bm7(♭5)
Esus4
you leave your key if I'd - 've known for just one sec - ond you'd be
-pect me to be free, now I'm sav - in' all my lov - in' for some
E
Am
Dm
back to both - er me. Go on now
one who's lov-in' me. Go on now
Go walk out the door just turn a-round

G
Cmaj7
Fmaj7
now 'cause you're not wel-come an-y- more. Weren't you the one who tried to hurt
Bm7(♭5)
Esus4
E
me with good-bye? Did I crum-ble, did you think I'd lay down and die? Oh no, not
Am
Dm
G
I. I will sur-vive, oh as long as I know how to love I
Cmaj7
Fmaj7
Bm7(♭5)
know I'll stay a-live. I've got all my life to live, I've got all my love to give and I'll sur-vive.

To Coda
Esus4
E
Am
Dm
I will sur-vive.
Hey, hey!
G
Cmaj7
Fmaj7
Bm7(♭5)
Esus4
E7
Am
2. It took all the strength I had not to
Dm
G
fall a-part, kept try-in' hard to mend the piec-es of my bro-

Cmaj7
Fmaj7
- ken heart; and I spent oh so man - y nights just feel - in'
Bm7(b5)
Esus4
E
D.S. al Coda
sor - ry for my - self. I used to cry, but now I hold my head up high. And you see
CODA
E
Am
Dm
Am
I'll sur - vive.

A Woman In Love

Words & Music by Barry Gibb & Robin Gibb

♩ = 84
E♭m
6fr
C♭maj7
D♭
4fr
N.C.
E♭m
6fr
C♭maj7
E♭m
6fr
A♭m
4fr
E♭m
6fr
A♭m
4fr
C♭
D♭
4fr
1. Life is a mo-ment in space; when the dream is gone, it's a lone-li-er place.
2. With you e-ter-nal-ly mine, in love there is no mea-sure of time.

G♭ D♭m C♭ E♭m A♭m7
I kiss the morn-ing good-bye, but down in - side
We planned it all at the start that you and I
B♭ E♭m A♭m
you know we nev-er know why. The road is nar-row and long
live in each oth-er's heart. We may be o-ceans a - way;
E♭m A♭m C♭ D♭ G♭
when eyes meet eyes and the feel-ing is strong.
you feel my love, I hear what you say.
D♭m G♭ C♭maj7 G♭ C♭maj7
I turn a-way from the wall; I stum-ble and fall, but I give you it all.
No truth is ev - er a lie; I stum-ble and fall, but I give you it all.
4fr 6fr

B♭7
E♭m
B♭7
E♭m
B♭7
I am a wo-man in love, and I'll do a-ny-thing
E♭m
B♭7
E♭m
B♭7
E♭m
to get you in-to my world and hold you with-in; it's a
D♭
A♭m
right I de-fend ov-er and ov-er a-
1.
G♭
E♭m
-gain. What do I do?

2.
C♭maj7
E♭m
6fr
What do I do?
B7
3
Oh,
Em
B7
I am a wo-man in love, and I'm talk-ing to you. I know how you feel
what a wo-man can do. It's a right I de-
D

Am
B
fend ov - er and ov - er a - gain.
Begin fade
Em
B7
Em
B7
Em
B7
I am a wo-man in love, and I'll do a - ny - thing to get you in - to my world
Em
B7
Em
D
Am
and hold you with - in; it's a right I de - fend
G
Em
ov - er and ov - er a - gain. What do I do?

The Winner Takes It All

Words & Music by Benny Andersson & Bjorn Ulvaeus

G♭
D♭/F
talk a - bout things we've gone through,
2. arms think - ing I be - longed there,
(Verses 3 & 4 see block lyric)
A♭m/E♭
though it's hurt - ing me, now it's his - to-
I fi - gured it made sense, build-ing me a
D♭
G♭
ry. I've played all my cards
fence, build - ing me a home,
D♭/F
and that's what you've done too, no - thing more to
think-ing I'd be strong there, but I was a

A♭m/E♭
D♭
say, no more ace to play.
fool, play-ing by the rules.
To Coda
G♭
B♭/D
The win-ner takes it all, the lo-ser stand-ing
The gods may throw a dice, their minds as cold as
E♭m
E♭/G
A♭m
small be-side the vic-to-ry,
ice, and some-one way down here
D♭
1.
that's her des-ti-ny.
lo-ses some-one dear.
2. I was in your

2.3.
G♭
B♭7/D
The win-ner takes it all, the lo-ser has to
The game is on a-gain, a lo-ver or a
E♭m
E♭/G
A♭m
fall, it's sim-ple and it's plain,
friend, a big thing or a small,
D♭
why should I com-plain?
the win-ner takes it all.
1.
2.
D.𝄋 al Coda
3. But tell me does she
4. I don't wan-na

CODA
G♭
B♭/D
E♭m
all.
E♭/G
A♭m
The win - ner takes it all.
D♭
G♭
B♭/D
E♭m
E♭7/G
A♭m

Verse 3:
But tell me, does she kiss like I used to kiss you,
Does it feel the same, when she calls your name?
Somewhere deep inside,
You must know I miss you,
But what can I say,
Rules must be obeyed.
The judges will decide the likes of me abide,
Spectators of the show always staying low.

Verse 4:
I don't wanna talk
If it makes you feel sad
And I understand you've come to shake my hand.
I apologise if it makes you feel bad
Seeing me so tense,
No self-confidence.
The winner takes it all.
The winner takes it all.

There Must Be An Angel (Playing With My Heart)

Words & Music by Annie Lennox & David A. Stewart

Dm7
G
this,
I'm thrown and ov - er - blown with
Instrumental
Am
G
F
bliss.
There must be an an - gel
G
Cm/E♭
Dm7
3
play - ing with my heart, yeah.
C
Dm7
1. I walk in - to an emp - ty room
2. And when I think that I'm a - lone

G
Am
G
and sud - den - ly my heart goes boom.
it seems there's more of us at home.
F
It's an or - ches - tra of an - gels
It's a mul - ti - tude of an - - - gels
G
Cm/E♭
To Coda
Dm7
and they're play - ing with my heart, yeah.
C
Fmaj7
Must be talk - ing to an an - gel,

A♭6
C
must be talk-ing to an an-gel,
must be talk-ing to an an-gel.
Fmaj7
A♭6
Must be talk-ing to an an-gel,
must be talk-ing to an an-gel,
C
Fmaj7
must be talk-ing to an an-gel.
Must be talk-ing to an an-gel,
A♭6
C
must be talk-ing to an an-gel,
must be talk-ing to an an-gel.

Am7
F
Must be talk - ing to an an - gel.
G7
Cm/E♭
Dm7
Must be talk - ing to an an - gel,
must be talk - ing to an an - gel.
1.
C
No-one on earth could feel like
2.
C
B♭
I must be hal - lu -
D7
Gm
3fr
- ci - na - ting, watch - ing an - gels ce - le - brat - ing.

B♭ D7 Gm
Could this be re-ac-ti-va-ting, all my sen-ses
B♭ D7
dis-lo-cat-ing. This must be a strange de-cep-tion,
Gm C7
by ce-les-tial in-ter-ven-tion. leav-ing me the
F G
re-col-lec-tion of your heav-en-ly con-nec-tion.
D.S. al Coda

Coda
C
Dm7
I walk into an empty room,
G
Am
suddenly my heart goes boom.
F
It's an orchestra of angels,
G
Cm/E♭
Dm7
they're playing with my heart. Yeah.

C
Dm7
Do da do da do da dun da, da
G
Am
G
da, da da.
F
G
Do da do da do da dun da, da da, da
Cm/E♭
Dm7
C
Repeat ad lib. to fade
da, yeah.
Harmonica

China In Your Hand

Words & Music by Carol Decker & Ronald Rogers

F♯ E B F♯/A♯ G♯m Gaug
man was in com-mand. It was a flight on the wings of a young girl's dreams that
child in the form of man. A pro-phe-cy for a fan-ta-sy, the
B6/F♯ E6 E6/F♯
flew too far a-way.
curse of a vi-vid mind.
E F♯ B F♯/A♯ G♯m G♯m/F♯
Don't push too far, your dreams are chi-na in your hand.
Instrumental
E F♯ D♯m E F♯
Don't wish too hard be-cause they may come true, and you can't help them.

E F♯ B F♯/A♯ G♯m G♯m/F♯
4fr 4fr
You don't know what you might have set up - on your - self, yeah,
E
To Coda
1.
F♯ B F♯ E
yeah: chi - na in your hand.
B F♯ E
2.
F♯ B F♯ E
2. Come chi - na in your hand, oh, your
D.S. al Coda
B F♯ E B
rit.
F♯ E B
hand, your hand.

Coda
F♯ E F♯ B F♯/A♯ G♯m G♯m/F♯
4fr 4fr
Don't push too far, your dreams are chi-na in your hand.
E F♯ D♯m E F♯
Don't wish too hard be-cause they may come true, and you can't help
E F♯ B F♯/A♯ G♯m G♯m/F♯
them. You don't know what you might have set up-on your - self, yeah,
E F♯
Repeat to fade
yeah. You just should-n't push too hard, no, no.

Eternal Flame

Words & Music by Susanna Hoffs, Tom Kelly & Billy Steinberg

B7
Em7
A7
To Coda
Do you feel the same? Am I on - ly
Do you feel the same? Am I on - ly
D
Bm7
1.
Am7
dream - - - ing, is this burn - ing
dream - - - ing or
2.
Am7
an e - ter - nal flame? is this burn - ing an e - ter - nal flame?
D
Dm7
G/D
D
Say my name, sun shines through the rain, a whole
f

F G C G/B Am7 Am/G
life so lone - ly and then come and ease the pain.
D Bm7 F/C C
1.
Dsus2 D
I don't wan - na lose this feel - ing, oh.
Em B7 Em A7 D Bm7
Am7
2.
Dsus2
D.%. al Coda
(Repeat verse 1)
oh.

Coda
D Bm7 Am7
dream - ing or is this burn-ing an e - ter-nal flame?
G Em7 C D G Em7
Close your eyes, give me your hand, darl - ing. Do you feel my heart beat-
f
C D7sus4 Em B7 Em7 A7
- ing? Do you un-der-stand? Do you feel the same? Am I on-ly
D Bm7 Am7
Repeat to fade
dream - ing, is this burn-ing an e - ter-nal flame?

Show Me Heaven

Words & Music by Maria McKee, Jay Rifkin & Eric Rackin

D♭ E♭ A♭ B♭ D♭ E♭
4fr 6fr 4fr 4fr 6fr
hold my hand don't let me fall you've such a-ma-zing
A♭ B♭ D♭ E♭ A♭ B♭m7
4fr 4fr 6fr 4fr
grace, I've ne-ver felt this way. Oh,
cresc.
f
D♭ E♭ A♭ B♭m7
4fr 6fr 4fr
show me hea-ven, co-ver me,
sim.
D♭ E♭ A♭ B♭m7
4fr 6fr 4fr
leave me breath-less. Oh,

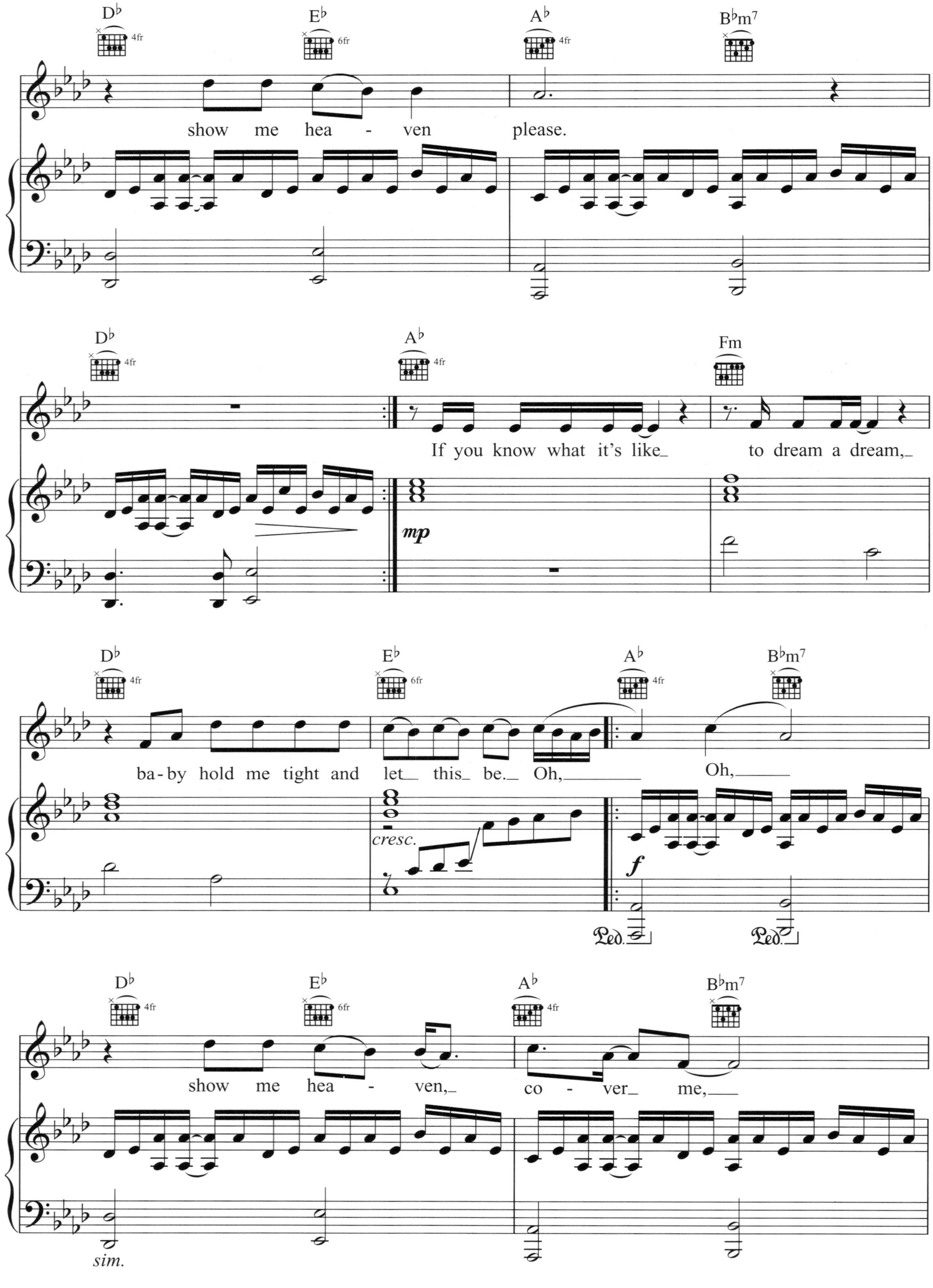
D♭ E♭ A♭ B♭m7
4fr 6fr 4fr
show me hea - ven please.
D♭ A♭ Fm
4fr 4fr
If you know what it's like to dream a dream,
mp
D♭ E♭ A♭ B♭m7
4fr 6fr 4fr
ba-by hold me tight and let this be. Oh, Oh,
cresc.
f
Ped. Ped.
D♭ E♭ A♭ B♭m7
4fr 6fr 4fr
show me hea - ven, co - ver me,
sim.

Verse 2:
Here I go, I'm shaking just like the breeze.
Hey babe, Ineed your hand to steady me.
I'm not denying I'm frightened as much as you.
Though I'm barely touching you,
I've shivers down my spine, and it feels divine.

Oh, show me heaven, *etc.*

Nothing Compares 2 U

Words & Music by Prince

F
C9sus4
F
C/E
3
Since U been gone I can do what - ev - er I want.
Dm7
F
C9sus4
F
I can see whom - ev - er I choose.
I can eat my din - ner in a fan - cy
C/E
3
Dm7
A7
res - tau - rant but no - thing, I said no - thing, can take a - way these blues. 'Cause
E♭
3fr
B♭
E♭
3fr
B♭
C
no - thing com - pares, no - thing com - pares 2 U.

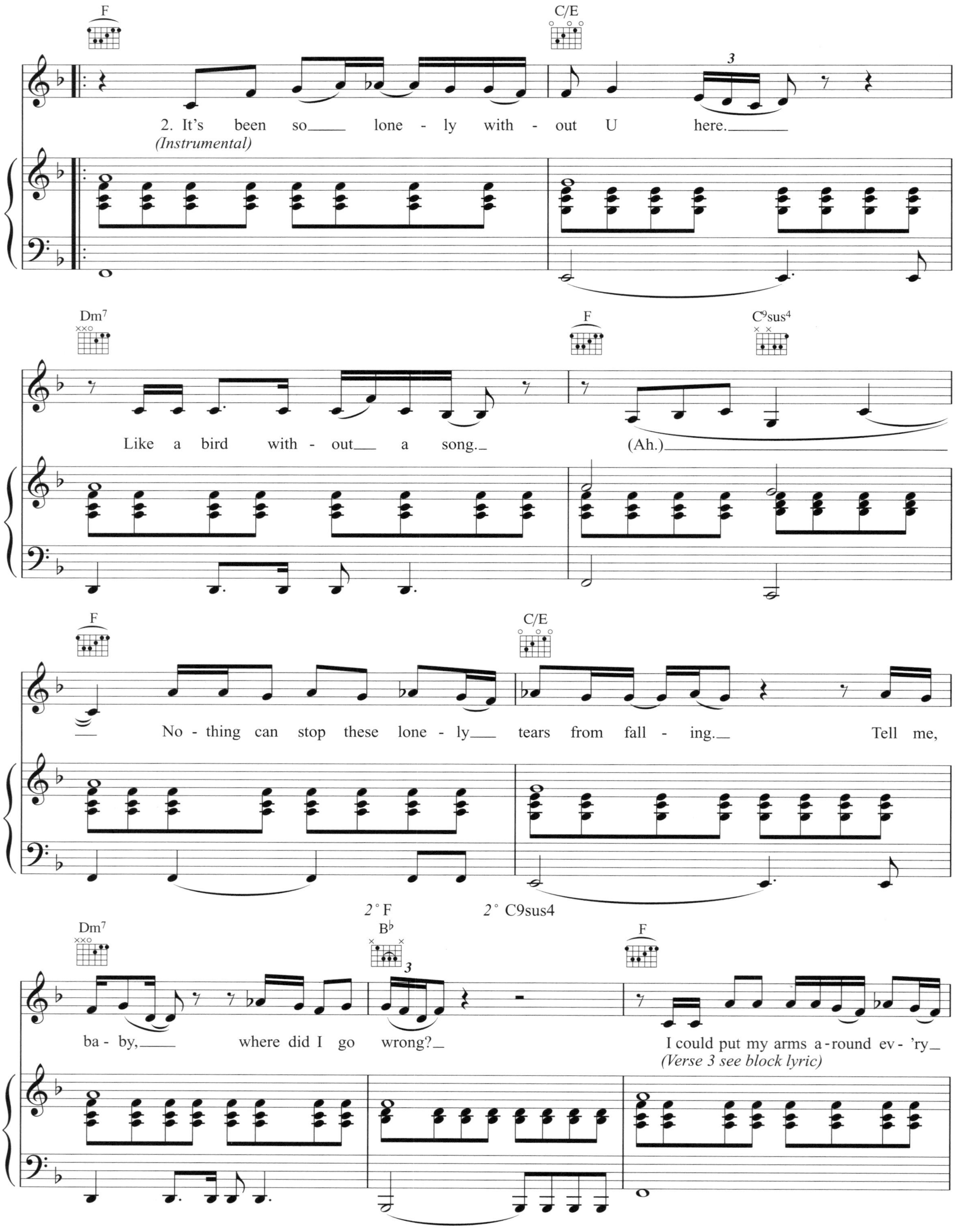
F
C/E
2. It's been so lone - ly with - out U here.
(Instrumental)
Dm7
F
C9sus4
Like a bird with - out a song.
(Ah.)
F
C/E
No - thing can stop these lone - ly tears from fall - ing.
Tell me,
2° F
2° C9sus4
Dm7
B♭
F
ba - by, where did I go wrong?
I could put my arms a - round ev - 'ry
(Verse 3 see block lyric)

C/E
Dm7
F
C9sus4
boy I see,
but they'd on - ly re - mind me of U.
(Ah.)
F
C/E
I went to the doc - tor and guess what he told me, guess what he told me. He said
Dm7
A7
E♭
3fr
B♭
"Girl U bet - ter try to have fun, don't mat - ter what U do." But he's a fool. 'Cause no - thing com - pares,
Dm
C
1.
no - thing com - pares 2 U.

Verse 3:
Instrumental
All the flowers that U planted Mama
In the back yard
All died when U went away
I know that living with U baby
Was sometimes hard
But I'm willing 2 give it another try.

Nothing compares, nothing compares 2 U *etc.*

I Will Always Love You

Words & Music by Dolly Parton

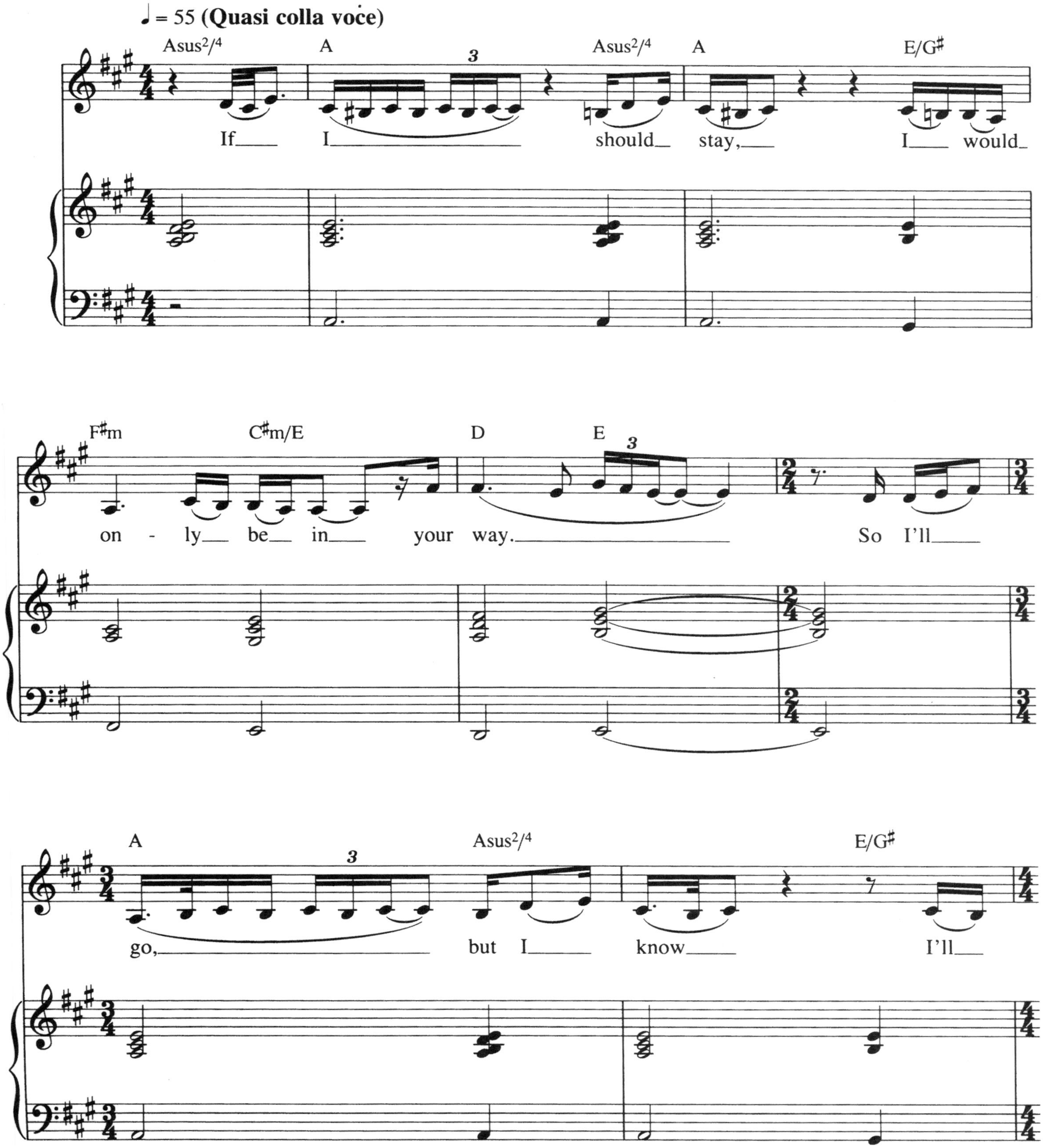

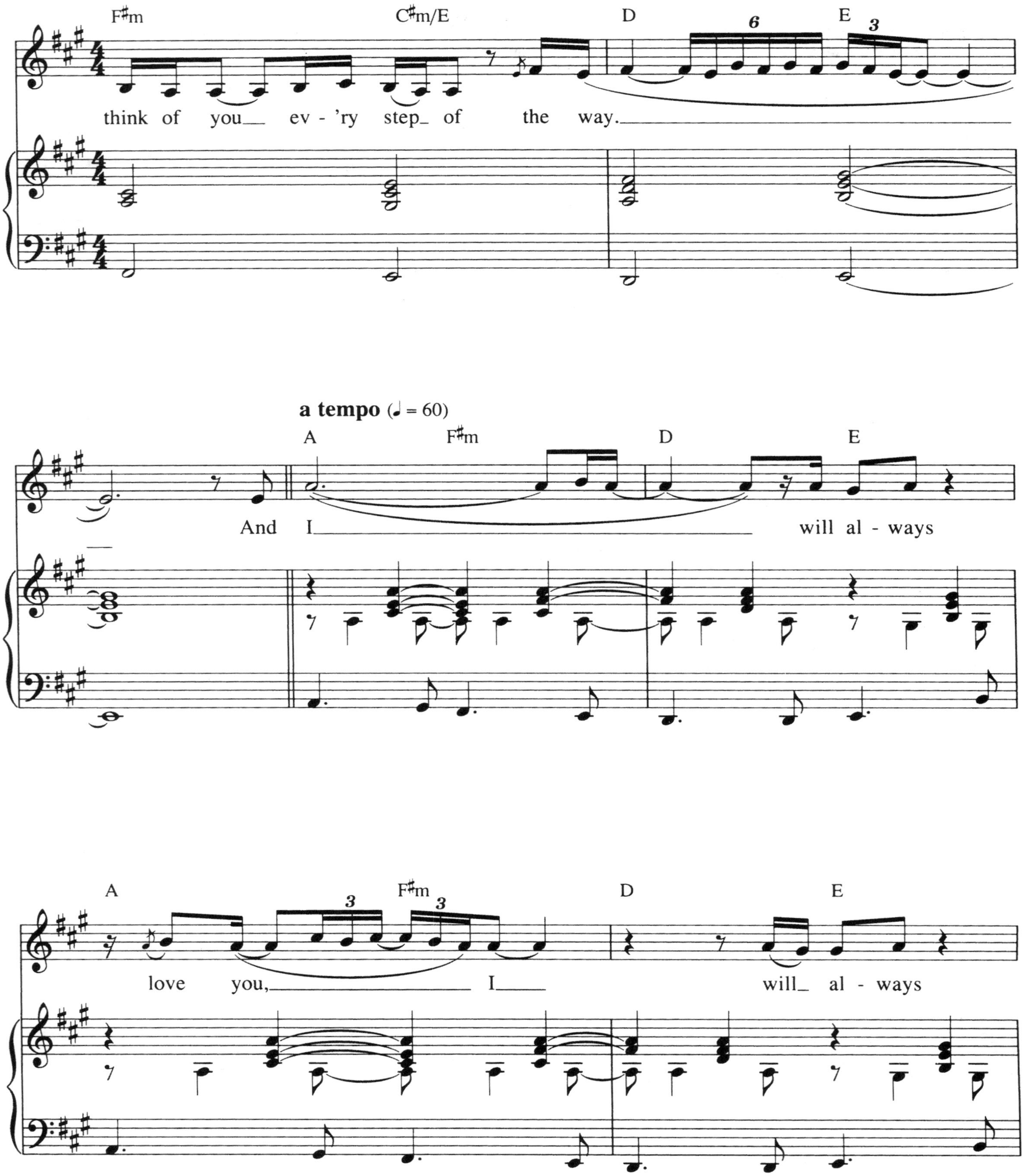
F♯m
C♯m/E
D
E
think of you ev - 'ry step of the way.
a tempo (♩ = 60)
A
F♯m
D
E
And I will al - ways
A
F♯m
D
E
love you, I will al - ways

poco accel.
A add9
D
love you,
you,
my
Amaj7/C#
Bm7
A/E
Esus4
dar - ling you,
mm.
Bit - ter -
a tempo (♩ = 67)
A
Asus2
Dadd9/A
A
Asus2
E/G#
F#m
C#m/E
- sweet me - mo - ries,
that is all I'm tak - ing with

D E A Amaj9 A A/G♯
me. So good-bye, please don't cry; we both
F♯m C♯m/E D E
know I'm not what you, you need. And I
A F♯m D E A F♯m
will al-ways love you, I
D E A D/A D/E A E6 E
will al-ways love you.

A D/A A E/G♯ F♯m C♯m/E
(1st time saxophone solo)
(2.) hope life_ treats you__ kind,_ and I__ hope___ you have all you dreamed
D E A Amaj9 A C♯m7
of.__ And I wish you joy_ and__ hap-pi- ness:___ but, a-bove all_
1. 2.
rit.
F♯m C♯m7/E Dmaj7 E Dmaj7 E
__ this, I___ wish you___ I__ love.___
a tempo
N.C. B G♯m E F♯
And I___ will al - ways_ love_
Drum beat

B G♯m E F♯ B G♯m
you, I will al - ways love you. I will al -
E F♯ B G♯m E F♯
ways love you. I I will al - ways love you.
B G♯m E F♯ B G♯m
I will al - ways lo - ve you,

rit.
Emaj7 F# G#m7add11 F#/A# N.C.
I, I will al - ways love
a tempo
E
you, you. Dar - ling I
molto rit.
Bmaj7/D# F#sus4 F# Badd9
love_ you._ Ooh,_ I'll al - ways, I'll_ al - ways_ love_ you.
Ped.
Ped.

Think Twice

Words & Music by Andy Hill & Pete Sinfield

♩= 72
F
Gm7
fr3
F
Gm7
fr3
Dm
Gm7
fr3
1. Don't think I can't feel that there's some - thing wrong,
(Verse 2 see block lyric)
C
Am7
B♭
you've been the sweet - est part of my life for so long.

Dm
3
Gm7
fr3
I look in your eyes, there's a dis - tant light
C
Am7
B♭
and you and I know there'll be a storm to - night.
Gm7
C
This is get - ting ser - i - ous,
Gm7
C
B♭/D
C/E
are you think - in' 'bout you or us. Don't say

F Bb C Bb/D C/E F Am7
what you're a-bout to say, look back be-fore you leave my
Bb C F Bb C
life. Be sure be-fore you close that door, be-fore you roll
Gm7 fr3
1.
Bb F
those dice, ba-by think twice.
Gm7 fr3
2.
Bb Dm
2. Ba-by think ba-by think twice.

Gm7 Dm7 Gm7
Gm7 B♭ C Gm7 B♭
Ba - by this is ser - i - ous, are you think-in' a-bout
C
you or us? Ba - by.
Don't say
F B♭ C B♭/D C/E
what you're a - bout to say, look back

Verse 2:
Baby think twice, for the sake of our love
For the memory,
For the fire and the faith
That was you and me.
Babe I know it ain't easy
When your soul cries out for higher ground,
'Cause when you're halfway up
You're always halfway down.

But baby this is serious
Are you thinking 'bout you or us?

...Baby One More Time

Words & Music by Max Martin

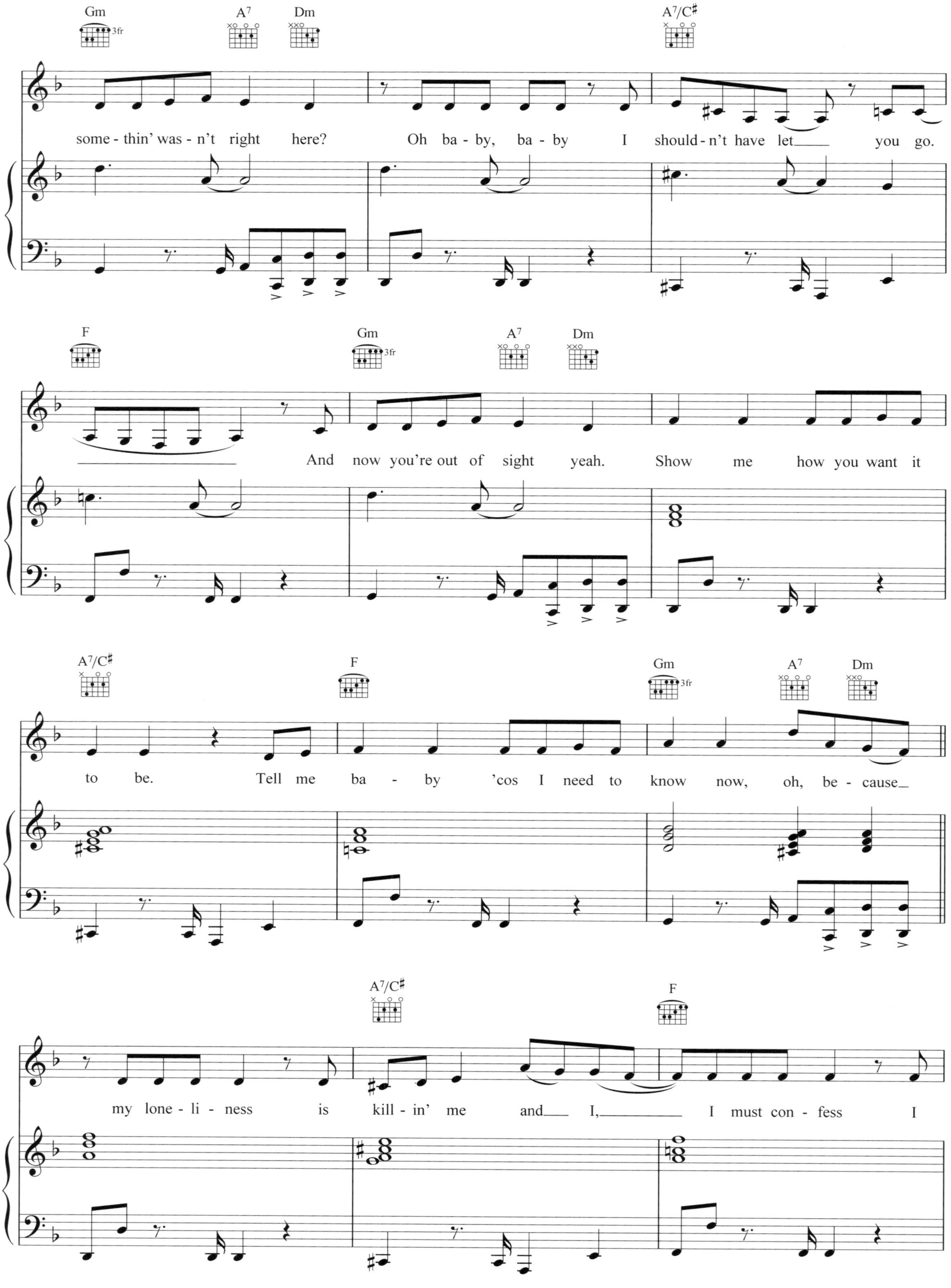
Gm A7 Dm A7/C♯
some-thin' was-n't right here? Oh ba-by, ba-by I should-n't have let you go.
F Gm A7 Dm
And now you're out of sight yeah. Show me how you want it
A7/C♯ F Gm A7 Dm
to be. Tell me ba-by 'cos I need to know now, oh, be-cause
A7/C♯ F
my lone-li-ness is kill-in' me and I, I must con-fess I

Gm Asus4 A Dm A7/C♯ B♭ C
still be - lieve, still be - lieve. When I'm not with you I lose my mind. Give me a sign,
F
1. Gm A7 Dm
hit me ba - by one more time.
2. Dm A Dm
hit me ba - by one more time.
Oh ba - by, ba - by. Oh, oh. Oh ba - by, ba - by. Ah yeah, yeah.
Dm A7/C♯ F/C
Oh ba - by, ba - by how was I sup - posed to know?

G♯m Asus4 A B♭ C
Oh pret - ty ba - by I should - n't have let you go.
Gm7 B♭ C Dm
I must con - fess that my lone - li - ness
A7/C♯ F Gm Asus4 A
is kill - in' me now, don't you know I still be - lieve
B♭ C B♭maj7 F/A Gm C A7/C♯
that you will be here and give me a sign. Hit me ba - by one more time.

Verse 2:
Oh baby, baby
The reason I breathe is you
Boy you got me blinded.
Oh pretty baby
There's nothing that I wouldn't do
It's not the way I planned it.

Show me, how you want it to be *etc.*

Don't Speak

Words & Music by Eric Stefani & Gwen Stefani

Gm7 Cm Fm7 B♭
can't be - lieve this could be the end. It looks
Cm Gm7 Fm7 B♭
as though you're let - ting go, and
we die both you and I
E♭ B♭ C
if it's real then I don't want to know.
with my head in my hands I'll soon be cry - ing.
Fm B♭m6 E♭ C
Don't speak, I know just what you're say - in', so please stop ex - plain -

B♭m6
C
Fm
B♭m
C
- ing, don't tell me 'cause it hurts.
Fm
B♭m6
E♭
C
Don't speak, I know what you're think - in', I don't need your rea -
B♭m6
C
1.
Fm
B♭m
E♭6
- sons, don't tell me 'cause it hurts.
Old
Cm
Gm7
Fm7
me - mo - ries, they can be in - vit - ing but some are

2.
B♭ Gm7 Fm7 B♭ Fm
fr3
all to-ge - ther might - y frighten - ing, As
D♭ A♭/C C♭ G♭/B♭
It's all end - ing, we've got to stop pre - tend - ing who we
A A(♭5) A♭ Cm Gm7
fr4 fr3 fr3
are.
Fm7 B♭ Cm Gm7 Fm7 B♭
fr3 fr3

Cm Gm7 Fm7 B♭
Gm7 Cm A♭ Fm9 Cm Gm7
You and me,
Fm7 B♭ Fm7 B♭
I can see us dying, aren't we?
Repeat with ad lib. vocals - 4° fade
Fm B♭m6 E♭ C
Don't speak, I know just what you're say - in', so please stop ex - plain-
(hurts.)

B♭m6 C Fm B♭m C
- ing, don't tell me 'cause it hurts.
Fm B♭m6 E♭ fr3 C
Don't speak, I know what you're think - in', I don't need your rea -
1, 3.
B♭m6 C Fm B♭m C
- sons, don't tell me 'cause it hurts. Don't tell me 'cause it
2.
Repeat ad lib. to fade
B♭m6 C Fm B♭m C
- sons, I know you're good, I know you're good, I know you're real good.

Perfect Moment

Words & Music by James Marr & Wendy Page

D♭ Fm D♭
God meant, this is my per-fect mo-ment with you.
Fm G♭maj9 fr3 B♭m
Wish I could freeze this space in time, the way that I
E♭m7 fr6 G♭m9 G♭m6 D♭
feel for you in - side. This is my mo-ment, this is my
3
Fm/A♭ D♭ Fm/A♭
per - fect mo - ment with you.

D♭add9 D♭ D♭maj7 D♭
2. Tell me you love me when you leave. You're more than a sha-dow,
D♭maj7 D♭add9 D♭ D♭maj7
that's what I be-lieve. You take me to pla-ces I nev-er thought I'd see.
D♭ G♭ E♭m7
Min-ute by min-ute you're the world to me. I wish I could frame the look in your
G♭maj9 B♭m Amaj7 F♯m6/A
eyes, the way that I feel for you in - side. This is my

D♭ Fm/A♭ D♭
mo-ment, this is my per-fect mo-ment with you.
C♭ G♭ D♭ C♭ G♭
And if to-mor-row brings a lone-ly day, here and now I know I
D♭ B♭m7 E♭m7 Fm B♭m7
have-n't lived in vain. No more tears in the rain, and if love nev-er comes a-gain I can
E♭m7 D♭/F E♭m7(♭5)/G♭ Amaj7 B/A
al-ways say I've been to pa-ra-dise skies in your eyes,

Amaj7
B/A
Amaj7
N.C.
eyes,
eyes.
D
Dmaj7
3. Tell me you love me the moment you leave.
D
Gmaj7
You're more than a sha - dow, I've got to be-lieve. I wish I could
Em7
Gmaj9
keep you all of my life, the way that I
3
3
3

Bm
B♭maj7
Gm6/B♭
feel for you in - side. This is my
D
F♯m/A
D
mo - ment, this is my per - fect mo - ment with you.
F♯m/A
A
D
F♯m/A
This is my mo - ment, this is my per - fect mo - ment with you,
Gmaj9
Gm
fr3
D
with you.

American Pie

Words & Music by Don McLean

Free time c. ♩= 68
A♭ Fm B♭m D♭
A long long time a - go I can still re - mem - ber how that
Fm E♭ A♭ Fm
mu - sic used to make me smile. And I knew that if I had my chance
B♭m D♭ Fm D♭/A♭ E♭
I could make those peo - ple dance and may-be they'd be hap - py for a while.

A tempo ♩= 104
E♭
fr3
A♭
fr4
B♭m
D♭
B♭m
1. Did you write the book of love and do you have faith in God above?
(Verse 2 see block lyric)
Fm
E♭
fr3
A♭
fr4
If the Bible tells you so.
Now do you believe in
Fm
B♭m
D♭
Fm
rock and roll and can music save your mortal soul, and can you teach me

B♭ E♭ E♭sus4 E♭
how to dance real slow? Well I
Fm E♭ Fm E♭
know that you're in love with him coz I saw you danc-in' in the gym. You
D♭ A♭/C B♭m D♭
both kicked off your shoes. Man I dig those rhy-thm and blues.
(Both kicked off your shoes.)
E♭ A♭ Fm B♭m
I was a lone-ly teen-age bronc-in' buck with a pink car-na-tion and a

D♭ A♭ E♭/G Fm
fr4 fr3
pick-up truck. But I knew that I was out of luck the day
D♭ E♭7 A♭ D♭ A♭ E♭
fr4 fr4 fr3
the mu - - sic died. I start-ed sing-ing
A♭ D♭ A♭ E♭ A♭ D♭
fr4 fr4 fr3 fr4
bye - bye Miss A - me - ri - can Pie. Drove my Che-vy to the lev-ee but the
A♭ E♭ A♭ D♭ A♭ E♭
fr4 fr3 fr4 fr4 fr3
lev - ee was dry. Them good ole boys were drink-in' whis-ky and rye sing-in'

Fm
B♭
Fm
To Coda
"This will be the day that I die. This will be the day that I
1.
E♭
E♭/D♭
A♭/C
E♭/B♭
E♭
E♭/D♭
A♭/C
E♭/B♭
die."
8vb
2.
E♭7
D.𝄋. al Coda
die."
Coda
E♭
E♭/D♭
A♭/C
E♭/B♭
E♭
E♭/D♭
die."
We start-ed sing-ing.

Verse 2:
I met a girl who sang the blues
And I asked her for some happy news
But she just smiled and turned away
Well I went down to the sacred store
Where I'd heard the music years before
But the man there said the music wouldn't play
Well now in the streets the children screamed
The lovers cried and the poets dreamed
But not a word was spoken
The church bells all were broken
And the three men I admire the most
The Father, Son and the Holy Ghost
They caught the last train for the coast
The day the music died
We started singing.

Bye-bye Miss American Pie *etc.*

Can't Get You Out Of My Head

Words & Music by Cathy Dennis & Rob Davis

♩= 130
Dm
Am
Dm
Am
(La la la la la la la la la la la la la la la la.)
Dm
Am
(La la la la la la la la la la la la la la la la.
I just

Dm
Am9
can't get you out of my head. Boy your lov - ing is all I
1° tacet
Dm
think a - bout. I just can't get you out of my head. Boy, it's
Am9
1.
2. 3.
more than I dared to think a - bout. think a - bout.
B♭maj7
A
G♯dim7
A
Ev - 'ry night, e - ve - ry day.
(2° see block lyric)

Gm7
3fr
Asus4
A
To Coda
Just to be there in your arms, Won't you
Dm
Am9
stay?
Dm
Won't you lay
Am9
B♭maj7
Stay for ev - er and

Am
D.%. al Coda
ev - er and ev - er and ev - er.
Coda
Dm
Am9
free.
Dm
Feel the need in
Am9
Dm
me Set me free.

Verse 2:
There's a dark secret in me
Don't leave me locked in your heart
Set me free *etc.*

Freak Like Me

Words & Music by Gary Numan, Eugene Hanes, Marc Valentine, Loren Hill, William Collins, George Clinton & Gary Cooper

♩= 92
C5
B♭5
3fr
1. Let me lay it on the line, I got-ta lit-tle
(Verse 2 see block lyrics)
frea-ki-ness in-side. And you know that a man has got-ta deal

N.C.
C5
B♭5
3fr
with it. I don't care what they say, I'm not a-bout to pay no-bo-dy's way, 'cause it's all
15ma
about the dog in me.
I wan-na
F5
freak in the morn-ing, a freak in the ev-en-ing. (Just like me.) I need a
rough-neck bro-ther that can sa-tis-fy me. (Just for me.) If you are

C5 3fr
B♭5
that kind of man 'cause I'm that kind of girl, I've got a
freaky secret ev'rybody sing 'cause we don't give a damn about a thing. 'Cause I will be a
freak until the day, until the dawn. And we can...
(pump) all through the night till the early morn. Come on and I will

C5 Bb5 C5 Bb5
3fr 3fr
take you 'round the 'hood on a gang - ster lean ___ 'cause we can...
C5 Bb5 C5 Bb5 C5 Bb5
3fr 3fr 3fr
1. 2.
(pump) a - ny time of day, 'sall good for me. ___ 2. Boy, ___ you're mov- (It's so good for me. ___
Gm F C Gm F
1. 2.
C C
(Good for me.) ___ I wan - na

Verse 2:
Boy you're moving kind of slow
You gotta keep it up now there you go
That's just one thing that a man must do
I'm packing all the flavours you need
I got you shook up on your knees
'Cause it's all about the dog in me.

I wanna freak in the morning *etc.*

Heaven

Words & Music by Bryan Adams & Jim Vallance

A♭
4fr
B♭
6fr
Cm
3fr
B♭
6fr
E♭/B♭
6fr
A♭
4fr
B♭
6fr
We're in hea - ven.
Cm
3fr
E♭
6fr
A♭
4fr
B♭
6fr
Cm
3fr
B♭
6fr

B♭sus4
E♭ Cm7 B♭sus4
1. Oh, think-ing a-bout our young-er years. There was
Fm7 Cm D♭ B♭sus4
on-ly you and me, we were young and wild and free.
E♭ Cm7 B♭sus4
Now no-thing can take you a-way from me.
2. Now no-thing can change what you mean to me.

Fm7
Cm
3fr
We've been down that road_ be- fore,_ that's
There's a lot that I_ could say_ but just
D♭
4fr
D♭/A♭
4fr
B♭sus4
ov - er now._ You keep me com - ing back for more._
hold me now,_ 'cause our love will light the way._
B♭
6fr
A♭
4fr
B♭
6fr
Cm
3fr
Ba - by you're all_ that I want when you're
E♭
6fr
A♭
4fr
B♭
6fr
ly - ing here_ in my_ arms. I'm find - ing it hard_ to be -

Cm
3fr
B♭
6fr
B♭sus4
lieve, we're in hea - ven. And
A♭
4fr
B♭
6fr
Cm
3fr
E♭
6fr
lov - ing is all that I need, and I've found it there in your
A♭
4fr
B♭
6fr
To Coda
Cm
3fr
heart. It is - n't too hard to see we're in hea -
B♭
6fr
1.
B♭sus4
- ven. We're in hea - ven.

2.
B♭sus4
Fm
Now our
E♭/G
A♭add9
B♭
dreams are com - ing true,
through the good times and the bad.
Cm
B♭
I'll be stand - ing there by you.
B♭sus4
B♭
B♭sus4
D.%. al Coda
We're in hea - ven.

Coda
Cm
B♭
E♭/B♭
we're in hea - - ven.
A♭
B♭
Cm
E♭
Oh, oh.
A♭
B♭
Cm
Oh, oh.
B♭
B♭sus4
N.C.
We're in hea - ven.
Drums

The Tide Is High (Get The Feeling)

Words & Music by John Holt, Bill Padley, Howard Barrett, Jem Godfrey & Tyrone Evans

Csus2
3fr
F
G
Csus2
not the things you do that tease and hurt me_ bad, but it's the way you do the things you
(Verse 2 see block lyrics)
F
G
Csus2
F
G
3
do to me. I'm___ not the kind of girl_ who gives up just___ like
C
F
G
C
F
G
that,___ oh no___ woh. The tide is_ high but I'm hold - ing on;
C
F
G
C
F
G
I'm gon - na be your_ num - ber one. The tide is_ high but I'm hold - ing on;

C F G Dm7 G
I'm gon-na be your num - ber one. Num - ber one.
My num - ber one.
Dm7 G G A
1. 2.
Num - ber one. (Whisper) Number one. one.
D G A
Ev - 'ry time that I get the feel - ing, you give me some - thing to be - lieve in.
D G A
Ev - 'ry time that I got you near me, I know the way that I want it to be.

D
G
3fr
A
But you know I'm gon - na take my chance now, I'm gon - na make it hap - pen some - how.
D
G
3fr
A
And you know I can take the pres - sure; a mo - ment's pain for a life - time's plea - sure.
N.C.
3
3
Ev - 'ry girl wants you to be her man,
Dsus2
3
but I'll wait right here till it's my turn. I'm not the kind of girl

Verse 2:
Every girl wants you to be her man
But I'll wait right here till it's my turn
I'm not the kind of girl who gives up just like that
Oh no.

Beautiful

Words & Music by Linda Perry

E♭7/D♭
Cm
B
wonderful, then suddenly it's hard to breathe.
-lirious, so consumed in all your doom.
E♭
E♭7/D♭
Cm
Now and then I get insecure from all the pain, I'm so a-
Trying hard to fill the emptiness, the pieces gone, left the puzzle
B
A♭
-shamed. I am beautiful, no
undone, is that the way it is? 'Cause you are beautiful, no
'Cause we are beautiful, no
Fm
E♭
E♭7/D♭
matter what they say. Words can't bring me down.
matter what they say. Words can't bring you down.
matter what they say. Yes words won't bring us down.

Cm
3fr
A♭
4fr
Fm
I am beau - ti - ful, in ev - 'ry sin - gle way. Yes,
You are beau - ti - ful, in ev - 'ry sin - gle way. Yes,
We are beau - ti - ful, in ev - 'ry sin - gle way. Yes,
E♭
6fr
E♭7/D♭
4fr
Cm
3fr
words can't bring me down. Oh, no.
words can't bring you down. Oh, no.
words can't bring us down. Oh, no.
Fm7
To Coda
1.
E♭
6fr
So don't you bring me down to - day.
E♭7/D♭
4fr
Cm
3fr
B

2.
E♭
6fr
E♭7/D♭
4fr
-day. No mat - ter what we do, no mat - ter what we say,
Cm
3fr
B
we're the song in - side the tune, full of beau - ti - ful mis - takes.
E♭
6fr
E♭7/D♭
4fr
And ev - 'ry - where we go, the sun will al - ways shine,
Cm
3fr
B
D.S. al Coda
but to - mor - row we might a - wake, on the oth - er side.

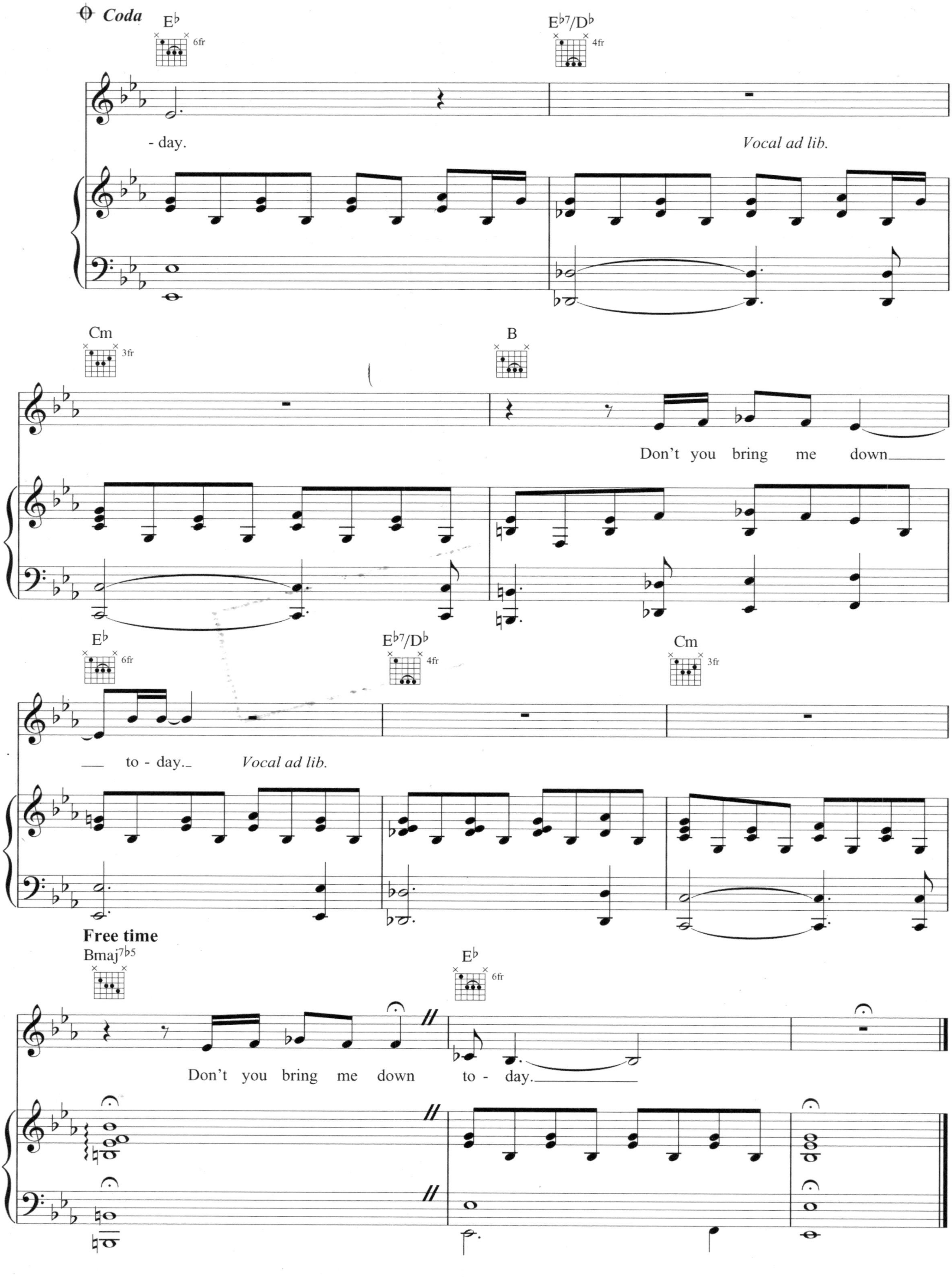

Printed in Malta by Progress Press Company Ltd. 3/06 (58427) - 2 3 4 5 6 7 8 9